'the republic of letters / a veritable la la land' writes Keri Glastonbury in *51 Alterities*, a collection in which cacophony rhymes with simplicity, and device notifications rebound across the desert horizon. In her poems 'nepo boys are punching above their weight', haunted by the 'spectres of unreal estate'; the senate estimate's axe 'falls in aggregates of joy' while budgies in their natural habitat have 'no idea they are suburban pretty boys'.

Glastonbury's previous collection *Newcastle Sonnets* was written as a riposte to Ted Berrigan's New York-based *The Sonnets*, and *51 Alterities* began too as a loose adaptation, of British poet Sam Riviere's influential 2012 debut *81 Austerities*. Riviere's collection was written in response to the impact of conservative austerity measures on the arts, and as a reconsideration of the function of poetry in the internet age. Wrestling with Antipodean 'alterity' more than ten years later, as a female queer poet a decade older than Riviere, Glastonbury's *51 Alterities* responds to the persistent threat of economic austerity, and to poetry's precarious place in a landscape dominated by billionaire tech bros and social media empires.

Cultural diarising and salty, gorgeous critique at its best; this poetry glides through and collapses time to bring us elegant bricolage that gathers, flips and spins... It's electric; slinging us observational side-eye, and stirring up glorious bite. Melinda Bufton

In these snappy poems, contemporary life is an experience of media, technology, celebrity and commercial debris of the twentieth and twenty-first centuries... Ironically, in affirming the oddness of it all, the collection may be grounding to those of us feeling washed out by the disorienting tides of the now. Prithvi Varatharajan

Other books by Keri Glastonbury

Grit Salute
Newcastle Sonnets

51 ALTERITIES

KERI GLASTONBURY

NEW POEMS

Published 2025
from the Writing and Society Research Centre
at Western Sydney University
by the Giramondo Publishing Company
PO Box 557
Willoughby NSW 2068 Australia
www.giramondopublishing.com

Cover and design by Jenny Grigg
Typeset by Andrew Davies
in Tiempos Regular 9/15pt

Printed and bound by Pegasus Media & Logistics
Distributed in Australia by NewSouth Books

A catalogue record for this book is available from the National Library of Australia.

ISBN: 978-1-923106-42-0

9 8 7 6 5 4 3 2 1

The Giramondo Publishing Company acknowledges the support of Western Sydney University in the implementation of its book publishing program.

This project has been assisted by the Commonwealth Government through Creative Australia, its arts funding and advisory body.

Alterity: otherness

specifically: the quality or state of being radically alien to the conscious self or a particular cultural orientation

Merriam-Webster

Contents

*

for over twenty years
I've considered
grants a fictitious form
of avuncular inheritance
an occasional cash cow
out to pasture at the (Les) Murray
(Robert) Gray stud
Bob's flashy sports car
Dorothy's wide forehead
her double denim
an antipodean Joplin

the republic of letters
a veritable la la land
failing sensitivity reads
on lux metres for small press
as poets take flight
like privileged pigeons
otherwise occulted
from the public square
she's the last person I'd expect
to be a cause célèbre
sending chills
down my trickster spine
at the vegan café
with a Buddhist monk
trembling into my almond milk
cappuccino with good art friends

is it the threat of accountability
or personalising now productivity
isn't just a dog whistle
from the right
writing a book of sonnets
and po-faced presenting them
to the vice-chancellor
as non-traditional research
blonde and profligate
choosing the right node to excise
fatigue wielding a soldering-iron
my poetic modus vivendi
wads of chewed-up paper
spat out a plastic pen
exclaiming like Tonks!
the cinema in poetry
belongs to her
O'Hara and Jorie Graham
we watch films on our devices
which even sounds suspect
like a beautiful cinematographer
shot dead by a stunt gun
capital in the Western desert

queer full-service sex workers
feed me vicarious popcorn
an Instagram AMA on cancel culture
citing Ayishat Akanbi
or an authentic Bellingen bildungsroman
John Waters or Emile Sherman
for the screen rights
forever falling down
the stairs in the Taxi Club
or posing under the Château Tanunda neon
homeless lying cheek by jowl
in the State Rail gloaming
deeper down a body weather lake
reverberating with echoes of Grotowski
Sydney post-departum
flashing a fishnet furphy

I am not an especially good
trauma counsellor
despite my Myers-Briggs 'J'
an inviolable divine
Clancy of the overshare
'for the word had passed around'
the cult of old regret

when Amazon runs fulfilment centres
in Arizona what's left for hustlers
in the time before
Fosseys became Target Country
Daisy Bates gone gonzo
lecturing the Karrakatta Club
on their original landladies
literary style is now a trojan horse
hiding in simple function words
the corpus cushioned
like a sequinned battering ram
with a Prince Albert piercing

the monument has no plaque
as if to say reputation
lasts as long as secret lemon-water writing
held up to the light
the communists and surf lifesavers
aligned against the riffraff
work is a form of everyday resignation
all the long-forgotten aldermen
Margel Hinder a footnote
on her fountain to Elon Musk on Mars

Ethereum sounds like it should be one of ours

**

Kupai sleeps on the bonnet of the Troopy
with all the intuitive charm of a dingo
howling on the service-provider strip

an anthropomorphism Kash Koolidge
could never depict

red dust creates a henna effect in your silver hair
as we drive into the centre of town on sunset
past the ice cream truck Mr Whippied over a ghost sign for fire
the mirage is like a recurring dream
that after raising a child my ex-partner from aeons ago
decides there's enough life left for a superannuated rekindling
yet I can't shake the feeling I'm trespassing
and wake to realise that you're sleeping beside me
otherworldly as that bisexual star of *Liquid Sky*
last night my boss decided to pull on the belt loops
of my jeans as a come-on which I appreciated
after a particularly desultory performance review
discharging wish fulfilment in my sleep
writing pink slips for maverick abandonment

somewhere a lost amphitheatre
for a trucked-in piano
playing a silent John Cage sonata
punctuated by an orange cuckoo clock
while Dolly Parton croons over wi-fi
calls for kungka remind me of
working in the Reasonably Good Cafe
and serving the Australia Council office workers
cappuccino in Redfern
a tarnished Airstream Silver Bullet glints
behind your military Perentie
papa lie patiently in the shade
we are all coining 'money story' for the arts
jumping in the truck for Weet-Bix
and exhibiting bush tomatoes
in the Lower East Side

it's possible to try to buy
the perfect outdoor gear online
but soaking in a cast-iron tub
by the spectral gum
with a few drops of bath milk
under the night sky
amplifies the *mise en abyme*
your breasts like flotillas
to test your eyesight
in a mirrorless selfie
until they too are light years away
and we are living
our daily sense data in situ

the decor is also traceable
to the source
even that puppy piss on the floor
is a mild inconvenience
the Petzl bag hanging
near the Seven Sisters
the means of production
nothing but a geolocator
like I can Google
to find out it was a fat bustard
we startled when driving
freeing the lizard
with its head stuck in a can of Coke
was my Bindi Irwin moment
I've got the Magpie Goose tank
sunglasses with yellow lenses
made from recycled ocean plastics
which really give the buffel grass
an incandescent glow

the graffiti in the one-room school   a scribbled plethora
of names   and outside the rock graves of two special boys
as a windmill   out the back   on the bore
with a broken pump   spins in fits and starts
the wind its body memory of utility/futility
the dry creek containing evidence   bracken swept up
from summer rain
        picking a cat's eye from your foot
without wince   in black skinny jeans
        with a bleached topknot   a lump of mingkulpa
lodged in your lower lip   cooler than an S.E. Hinton greaser
driving home dozy past the bogged Bedford
with a rusty wang   playing *Pink Moon*

chrysoprase green in the rocks
the shadow of my legs cast over
red boulders as I imagine myself
in Marfa Texas with a car wreck
installed on polished concrete or
Taos New Mexico with Agnes aging
again in mortal gridlock swimming
dissipating laps as the council
demolishes the chalky numbered
blocks that stood in Sesame Street
certainty until you stop counting
or this birthday cook a kangaroo
tail in the coals with Melbourne
millennials opening like a skylight
at the Guggenheim Bilbao the glass
on consignment at the Jam Factory

life trajectories incorporating missionaries and sepia-toned photographs careful or you'll be backed over under a tree lying there so ethereally as if the past can postpone tragedy and the red turns a certain orange that rises to meet the intensity of intelligent design not even a screen could ever be that vivid as the radiator boils over somewhere out past Wingellina and the nyi nyi birds lead the women to water a photo of Snow Dog and her owner in a leopard-skin coat and beanie turning off to the tip (Bunnings)

it clouds over as Bon Iver
plays on the UE Boom
like a set piece far from Illinois
call out to Miranda to join us on a walk
in the evening storm
wearing my felt Will + Bear fedora
various assemblages of rocks
on the hills beckon
I'm getting Laura Ingalls Wilder vibes
in SÜK pants with waist adjustors
as the new corsetry

there it is the moon
a tatty piece of calico
water flowing incongruously
in the roadside ditch
while you dance
like Gene Wilder
without a pole
for my Insta reel
and we're all so pasty
like Clag my hair thick with it
trying to find
the right Dr Bronner's dilution
a cameo in a Camus story
about a woman
in the Algerian desert

my first and only foray
into Western Australia
is Irrunytju where *Tracks* was filmed
I'm in awe of Robyn and Diggity
and Bruce too though he's outside
my bandwidth of aesthetic acumen
I wonder if they knew each other
through Salman (stabbed)
and if Bruce knew Andy (shot)
through Robert (we've been watching
The Diaries on Netflix)
the deepfake voiceover
is an actorless adjudicator
another psychoanalysis of shame
which I didn't quite buy
or for Robyn either
as if *National Geographic*
was queerbaiting

a Judas collar on a journalist
and a camel called Goliath
kneeling in Sufi split-screen
visions of an electric wheelchair derby
for elders doing burnouts
the real sky news broadcasting after dark
circling like a wedgetail with bait in its guts
the senate estimate's axe
falls in aggregates of joy
igniting a séance of workplace grievance
flicking biros like lightsabres
mooning as arts activism
the old model is the trusted vehicle
that Whitlam rolled out
until he was rolled out
self-inseminating on the public purse

three weeks in a twinkling town
enough for city lights
out the plane window to be defamiliar

the Luna Park face soothing and terrifying
the child in me all that out there
the maleficent cloak I wear

slipping back in like every other random
my car refusing to reverse out of the long-term
carpark as if wheel-clamped

wearing a sadomasochistic hood
advertising lesbian Renault
handbrake hypervigilance

spongy with El Niño moisture
gaslit in a Botany noir
an indubitable monologue

on the back streets of Enmore
cars wedged like bared teeth
a Cold Chisel Saturday Night (do do do etc.)

I'm dying for Faheem's like any taxi driver
the antipathy everlasting
and mutual (open up your gizzards)

a metallic shucking in the rear
yes I know how to live variously
more than that spew on the footpath

hello King Street 'you talking to me'
it's been a while since
your vibe tribe parties at the brickworks

people are (house) deposited here
now and cramming it in dankly
ibis surveilling Inner West wetlands

occupying a nature strip
watching oldies drive past and ostracise
the dog stranded saintly

tapping onto a train in Epping
perilously snaking
a backtrack through the Hawkesbury

shark-like headlights on the motorway
teenagers on their phones
pierced Centy Coast boys kiss softly

breathing in gingivitis under this face mask
a Christian college kid mouthing off
about gender in the quiet carriage

behind us
the lone palm
of Jerusalem Bay

***

I was in an aisle
    in Mayfield Woolworths
        throwing things in my basket
    disavowing you
had the shits at your antics
    called a gronk
        by one of your associates
    and thought
they were calling
    me a gonk
        you know those fake-fur
    covered tin cans
with googly eyes
    I'll take it
        as a compliment

what would Thoreau make of Riparide
the people in the window at Goldbergs
must be made of wax by now
or sticky date pudding
an expense table buggered
by the cost of perishables
at the Pipalyatjara store
why walk at all when there's no pond
Wordle's graphic equaliser populates feeds
like morse code used to travel
the Telstra Track
see Derryn Hinch's guide
in the bargain book basement
you've almost stopped buying food
which I now see has been an ulterior motive
tiny squares of grass as a colour-field artwork
budgies in their natural habitat
no idea they are suburban pretty boys

capable of hitting the accelerator
instead of the brake at any age
the Camira I drove
into the front brick fence
of Grandview Avenue
now someone's slammed into the BP servo
hives are poisoned due to varroa mite
and vernacular architecture is reprised
after the floods at the dog beach
a different depression era
farting discreetly out on the breakwall
Mavis Beacon taught me to touch-type
now I hear a horse and cart
in the time before
this person does not exist
there was a real face model
smattered with tattooed freckles
the demographic I left a decade ago
starts calling me out
a pleasant shock at who succeeds
on OnlyFans getting their growler out

I would like to rock
chronic sand erosion
priced out of property
gentrifier as a verb
a limpet that clung
to their superannuation
rounded-vowel landlords
refusing to let tenancy
destroy the poetics
of a bathroom window
staring out to sea
like *The Ghost and Mrs Muir*
spectres of unreal estate
somehow comes down to patience
and erotic taxation
a pejorative
which for others is a prerogative
asphyxiation fantasies
simple as mock dentistry
and poor suction
thinking about my greyhound's snoot
to self-soothe in the chair
and why I can never orgasm
with socks on

who knew it's trebled not tripled
we found out over a vegetarian burger
like the local radio station
enlightened me about a pineapple
on the Wimbledon trophy

two tiny ceramic triangles
one pink one blue
in my ears

a Split Enz album cover
on a t-shirt in a bargain bin

the shaved bits a signifier
the ugliest pair of purple
Doc Martens

that poster of Leonardo DiCaprio
from *The Face*
I used to keep inside
my wardrobe
looking like a baby dyke

a minuscule piece of
the teenage never never

vs. poetry that J.D. Vance would consider an Appalachian obituary
vs. poetry that J.T. LeRoy would consider blowing at a truck stop
vs. poetry that k.d. lang would consider jonesing
vs. poetry that J.K. Rowling would turf
vs. poetry that Louis C.K. would consider creepypasta
vs. poetry that O.J. Simpson would consider appealing
vs. poetry that R.F.K. Jr would consider heavy metal
vs. poetry that T.S. Eliot would consider over-amped
vs. poetry that H.P. Lovecraft would consider tentacle porn
vs. poetry that P.G. Wodehouse would drip marmalade on
vs. poetry that A.D. Hope would consider spiritually bloated
vs. poetry that A.S. Byatt would throw side-eye
vs. poetry that e.e. cummings would consider over-capitalised
i.e. poetry that *is* a 'HOT TEXTUAL OBJECT'
vs. poetry that C.S. Lewis would consider IKEA
etc....

L'Avventura is about ennui
now Grammar graduates'
photos are endless
in the way that Italy and Majorca
remind me of James Bond films
these nepo boys are punching
above their weight
backflipping off various viaducts
more big fish small pondage
nostalgia for the old Northern Beaches
it's the scrolling that keeps it plotless
and the drone footage in perspective
personified by a kind of coy friendliness
that means yes we surf and jet ski
and our drinks are classics
on ice not in bogan beer fridges
in the man cave and we can
definitely catch a chairlift
in our anoraks with big smiles
global-warming anxiety aside
we're bringing back the
rat pack with a social conscience
the brat pack is just cringe

I plod along seeking content
that I don't share because
I'm well able to perform
to an audience of one
my gene pool ends here
no summer festivals enticed
me into a cowgirl costume
my brain-cell damage
from whatever undiagnosed
chronic condition du jour
lends itself to experimental
poetry and the brief conscious
seconds of noticing
that might be all
we ever extract of
ourselves in place
asemic coal seams
my phone edits
reels for me now
my private Idaho
becoming my own
public Nevada
that flickering pull
on the bowser
too late to rescind

following Brittany
humanises us all
we are psych wards
tattooed across knuckles
like Diamanda Galás
diseases accumulate
the inflammation
the long Covid
the mastectomies
the ovarian scans
the prostate gardening
and I think of Björk
and poets lying
while televisions create magic
those stealthy Lilliputians
tie shibori knots on tech bros
encrypting safe words
as diodes fry and frazzle
and the poem makes
them function again briefly
custodians of micro datasets
distillers of craft spirits
tiny homes of trepidation
semiotic misconduct
in closed circuits

the multiple things
that happen in reality
will come out in the wash
even if you were drunk
as a skunk and cannot testify
as a sovereign subject
the Matildas players say
they plan to leave it
all out on the field
not a fleck of bias
in the upholstery
shrinking in the spin
cycle of legacy media
soft spittle spluttering
like twenty-cent agitations
along a newsagent scratchie
a chancer's soft cock
betting the farm
swathed in autofill
autocratic rare earths
gouging hip flexors
perplexing fatbergs
salty as a bovine lick
mired in discord channels
a noise-cancelling climax

not being one of Antonioni's mega-rich
I did dream about meat pies
like they weren't fattening

sook harder softballer

I'm lying on memory foam
with a mattress protector
used in aged care
wasn't the best sales pitch
and all the sex toys trade off ideas from
articles on my phone about sugar babies
a form of last drinks or intel
I claim from being bent in the 90s
the vertiginous anxiety
of trying to verbalise sexual pleasure
is a lot like aphantasia
the monitor isn't plugged in
the hard drive is still thrumming
and somehow the vectors deliver
porn hiccuping over dial-up
or all the televisions at Bing Lee going at once
like silenced pound dogs

sport is the electrometer of Australia
which means we don't really need tutorials
except for tutorials that understand they are excess
to requirement which leads to courses
like peak poetry
every time I hear the word lockdown
I think of *Oz* and how soapy it ultimately became
which leads to courses like peak TV
Queer As Folk now blowing meth smoke
there's no way to teach you this in real time
unless you were watching the tennis that summer
and wearing a Where Is Peng Shuai t-shirt
the Russian foreign minister sitting
in Bali wearing a ~~Bintang~~ Basquiat t-shirt

goodnight John-Boy
where does your family sit
on *The Waltons'* trauma scale
the opportunity to talk to grandfathers
is something that is lost but mid-century
as an aesthetic is perhaps less brutal
more Facebook Marketplace
my next-door neighbour in primary school
had an op-shop men's shirt and I guess
this is still kids though even that movie
has an essay now that old smell of must
as things distinguish in both senses
somehow shoehorned into family geometries
like that Tupperware Shape-O
and a fear of engulfment
don't mention the Norris Nuts'
latest Bondi real estate ventures
as Drunk Elephant sells out at Mecca
I'm bereft of a teenage daughter
but pathetically across it

I've been to The Anglers Rest
and developed a photograph
in a darkroom
heard the carnal knowledge
argument but had no real idea
sailing up to Brooklyn
after I met a poet
at Writers in the Park
staggering into the toilets
after walking from Cowan
give me Timothée Chalamet
and I'm singing along in the cinema
the genre purists still admirably
packing up the folding chairs
just don't jump on the back of that Triumph
Lana Del Rey is coming
I appreciate the knack
I just can't emulate it
it would be like top surgery
in *Vale Street* (1975)
leaving the ankh

I told my gay neighbour
I wasn't doing anything
but then went and ate a whole packet
of pride Oreos from Coles
and felt celebratory and sick

this poem is like the Netflix adaptation
of *The Lost Daughter* not Italian enough
though who's to say that opera
isn't played in housing commission
that you can't celebrate your son's ex
posting a lesbian thirst trap
I really hated that guy in *Normal People*
he liked Frank but didn't have an ounce of camp
we rarely sit on the couch to watch TV
moving the plush dog bed

when so much is in abundance
so much is also scarce
though female vox revives
Leonard Cohen on substrates of oilier and oilier rags
while *The Guardian* racks up comments
we still have *our* aperçu right
poetic blockchains bristling with iron filings
like a magnet under paper

if this is the internet in its infancy
then why isn't it cooler
like the analogue world used to be
now cat memes are getting me
fifteen years after I got out of the shower
harkening back to a temporality
that the moment contains in multitudes
who needs jocular radio announcers
or even communal listening pleasure
in a world of no duds and no repeats
and adult back-tickles towards retirement
remember *Harold and Maude*
when the prevailing idea
of youth resilience
seemed sad and anti-punk
nobody wants to be a bad ancestor
to let the humanities down
with a low-taper fade
conceding in the opening stanza

I can't quite fathom
writing poems about
the Sweet New Style
though I register them
as a mode of accrual
a spongy carpet underlay
sotto voce
what is lost when ethnographers
turn to arts-based methods
rather than endlessly
debating Dennis O'Rourke
documentaries
our discussions in the Valhalla
mired in lifelong yearning
sweet days of ingenuity
where are those thirteen-year-olds now
in the 'connie' cardigans
it's all still high-waisted not -minded
who on the ham-fisted board
didn't realise it's a poem
not literally about stone fruit
and the theme of discovery
pea-picking criticism
and culpability

I'd prefer to be
rescuing Kosci brumbies
though I care about peat moss
and corroboree frogs
burnt sugar pines
at Laurel Hill
(which I always mix up
with Laurel Canyon)
and so much music
on mixtapes
seeped in
to the Land Cruiser
floating like a corpse
in the freezing blue waterhole
in that way that Brandi Carlile
is just so American
and Martha Wainwright
is saved by being Canadian
let's start by
all asking ourselves

should we really duet
or not

she's buying Duckfeet to 'Anthem'
mum's on the walls variously iterated
while you holiday at Heron Island
and baby turtles wish for 100 years
dad's trying açaí at eighty
and reading about the Anthropocene
write me a poem in the style of Dan Hogan
that draws on the philosophies of Monique Wittig
is there a slope card I can put underneath
or one of those rubber pen grips
to correct my grasp
I've googled Liz Grosz
to check my undergraduate
understanding of sexual difference
and need to start back-pedalling fast
the crack is ontological
Cate Blanchett is way more than a muse
but even she doesn't have the answers
she thinks she does

the sun streaming through
like data from a crepuscular cloud
reading Marguerite Duras
proactively in case of class umbrage
let's discuss the homo*sek*sual friend motif
Hemingway's becoming a man in 'Indian Camp'
and S.J. Norman's 'Stepmother'
I even said poets could slow down time like Tár
that enjambment is glitching
the b almost onomatopoeic
as the students look politely bereft
like The Press Bookhouse is bereft of Dransfield
though the library still has *Drug Poems*
and the local greyhounds are called Paloma and Portia
I dedicate this lecture to the thinking woman's crumpet

****

what can I suggest we do instead
I'm not saying anyone should stop
give up and find a job...
Sam Riviere, 'And There the Resemblance Ends'

it's not lost on me
this irony that is sharing
a tiny ounce of self
is the equivalent
problem in prose

I can't even
and some young
poet in New Zealand
called Hera
has already said it better

the decades are available
to all now even
the Bladerunners
are getting soggy
in the endless
city rain

nurses study so they
can give injectables
people click like
to try to force
forward momentum
Billie Eilish eyes
lower their F-stop
and the last millisecond of a voice note
asks me to guess

it's not auteurism
autism or an aneurysm
but when people say
something spontaneous
we stop still for a second

generate a mixture
of the felt and the random
in a staccato
style that might be
a memoir of this moment
while world cups are won
by mere deflection

Starlink satellites spoof glitter
across Carly Simon's Bluesky
more sprogs on the event horizon
while literary acquisitions creep
like blue-green algae
exiting the Anglosphere
I tell you the poem isn't even
about you and you say cloud cover
but mean archive

Ghislaine drawing the court artist
a bad pet portrait
of someone's sausage dog
or the extreme cake
of presidential pardons
another baby reindeer
covered in snowflakes

reclaiming unhinged mode
to bust through task paralysis
in these febrile times
without sounding too much
like an arts-adjacent CEO
teetering along a glass cliff

when lacking in doubt
is a fortified wind turbine
strong statements
by Penny Wong
stoic nostalgia
it's impolitic to say
I'm seventy-three per cent sure
the whales have dyscalculia

alterity sounds like
a whiff of cologne
when I type the word crisis
I don't mean my own mid-life
or that the supermarket
is out of eggs again

five-day weather forecasts
are like mood-swings
mild tomorrows tip me into
more salad days
hunger a quiet unanswered
message in my body

I see Barron Trump has
really shot up
must be sponsored
by a protein powder
Joe Biden in aviators
his masculine voice tinny
out an airport tannoy
when he said it might be
the other team like he was
watching the Super Bowl

if a man breaks down in the UK
over the decline
of Land Rover Defenders
nobody calls it hysteria
they just adjust their cufflinks
and read more Wilfred Owen
in America it involves more weapons
both distrust spoken word nights
a battle between Riviere
and Bukowski
one says leitmotifs
the other something
about a prostitute
in '72

what's not to know is what's missing
public secretions not visible
unless desecration of form
tells us what we hold sacred in any spiel
tone policing the tariffs
of your censors/senses
with Isemonger's
asphodels/infidels

Putricia parsing the patience
of her pollinator
Eleanor playing backgammon
in Dr Dark's cave
Montaigne in his castle
with the pigs

the essay I wish I wrote

eshay! sashay!
work it

Sincerely, K. Glastonbury

Acknowledgements

This collection is offered as a loose 'antipodean' adaptation of Sam Riviere's *81 Austerities* (Faber and Faber, London 2012) which he wrote in response to the impact of austerity measures on the arts and as a provocation on poetry as a contemporary media in the internet age. I wanted to wrestle with the axis of genre, gender and generation as a female queer poet over a decade older, and now over a decade on, in an era of increasing tech broligarchy.

51 Alterities was partly written on Anangu Pitjantjatjara Yankunytjatjara (APY) Lands as a guest of Ninuku Arts. Always was, is and will be.

This project has been assisted by the Australian Government through Creative Australia, its arts funding and advisory body, the Copyright Agency's Cultural Fund, the University of Newcastle, and Varuna, The National Writers' House.

I am grateful to the editors of *Cordite POP!*, *Coastlines* and *The Chalamet Review* where earlier versions of poems in this collection have been previously published.

Notes

1. Epigraph p. v
'Alterity.' Merriam-Webster.com Dictionary, Merriam-Webster, https://www.merriam-webster.com/dictionary/alterity. Accessed 26 February 2025

2. 'I am not an especially good' p. 7
Paterson, A.B. 'The Man from Snowy River.' *The Man from Snowy River and Other Verses*, Sydney University Press, 2009, p. 3.

3. 'on the back streets of Enmore' p. 26
Walker, Don. 'Saturday Night', performed by Cold Chisel, *Twentieth Century* WEA, 1984.
Travis Bickle asks 'You talking to me?' in *Taxi Driver*. Directed by Martin Scorsese, Columbia Pictures, 1976.

4. 'vs. poetry that J.D. Vance would consider an Appalachian obituary' p. 37
The line 'i.e. poetry that *is* a "HOT TEXTUAL OBJECT"' cites Sam Riviere's 'Loosely Spiritual American Poetry', *81 Austerities*, London, Faber and Faber, 2012, p. 34.

5. 'it's not lost on me' p. 57
Riviere, Sam. 'And There the Resemblance Ends.' *81 Austerities*, London, Faber and Faber, 2012, p. 11.

6. 'what's not to know is what's missing' p. 62
The lines 'eshay! sashay! / work it' are riffs off RuPaul's 'Supermodel (You better work)', *Supermodel of the World,* Tommy Boy Records, 1993.
The line 'Sincerely, K. Glastonbury' is a riff off Leonard Cohen's line 'Sincerely, L. Cohen' from 'Famous Blue Raincoat', *Songs of Love and Hate,* Columbia Records, 1971.

7. Lines in italics in Section Four were generated using fragments from GPT-4 prompting.

About the Author

Keri Glastonbury is Associate Professor in Creative Writing at the University of Newcastle. Her poems have been widely published in magazines and collections. She has been the recipient of the Australia Council's BR Whiting Residency in Rome and an Asialink Literature Residency in India. Her poetry collection *Newcastle Sonnets* was published by Giramondo in 2018, and shortlisted for the 2019 Prime Minister's Literary Award for Poetry. Her previous collections include *Grit Salute* (Papertiger, 2012).